My Feelings Diary

_____

_____

_____

DATE:................

SOMEONE THAT HELPED
ME TODAY...

THREE GOOD THINGS
ABOUT TODAY....

1

2

3

ONE WORRY I HAVE IS....

I Score Today...

$\overline{10}$

My Feelings Today.

5	
6	
7	
8	
9	
10	
11	
12pm	
1	
2	
3	
4	
5	
6	
7	
8	

Extra Notes:

DATE:...............

SOMEONE THAT HELPED
ME TODAY...

THREE GOOD THINGS
ABOUT TODAY....

1

2

3

ONE WORRY I HAVE IS....

I Score Today...

10

My Feelings Today

5	
6	
7	
8	
9	
10	
11	
12pm	
1	
2	
3	
4	
5	
6	
8	

Extra Notes:

DATE:...............

SOMEONE THAT HELPED ME TODAY...

TODAY I FEEL:

THREE GOOD THINGS ABOUT TODAY....

1

2

3

ONE WORRY I HAVE IS.....

I Score Today...

$\dfrac{}{10}$

My Feelings Today

5	
6	
7	
8	
9	
10	
11	
12pm	
1	
2	
3	
4	
5	
6	
8	

Extra Notes:

DATE:...............

SOMEONE THAT HELPED
ME TODAY...

TODAY I FEEL:

THREE GOOD THINGS
ABOUT TODAY....

1

2

3

ONE WORRY I HAVE IS....

I Score Today...

—
10

My Feelings Today

5	
6	
7	
8	
9	
10	
11	
12pm	
1	
2	
3	
4	
5	
6	
7	
8	

Extra Notes:

DATE:..............

SOMEONE THAT HELPED ME TODAY...

TODAY I FEEL:

THREE GOOD THINGS ABOUT TODAY....

1

2

3

ONE WORRY I HAVE IS....

I Score Today...

—
10

My Feelings Today.

5	
6	
7	
8	
9	
10	
11	
12pm	
1	
2	
3	
4	
5	
6	
7	
8	

Extra Notes:

DATE:...............

SOMEONE THAT HELPED ME TODAY...

THREE GOOD THINGS ABOUT TODAY....

1

2

3

TODAY I FEEL:

ONE WORRY I HAVE IS....

I Score Today...

10

My Feelings Today

5	
6	
7	
8	
9	
10	
11	
12pm	
1	
2	
3	
4	
5	
6	
7	
8	

Extra Notes:

DATE:...............

SOMEONE THAT HELPED ME TODAY...

THREE GOOD THINGS ABOUT TODAY....

1

2

3

TODAY I FEEL:

ONE WORRY I HAVE IS....

I Score Today...

10

My Feelings Today

5	
6	
7	
8	
9	
10	
11	
12pm	
1	
2	
3	
4	
5	
6	
8	

Extra Notes:

DATE:...............

SOMEONE THAT HELPED
ME TODAY...

THREE GOOD THINGS
ABOUT TODAY....

1

2

3

TODAY I FEEL:

ONE WORRY I HAVE IS....

I Score Today...

$\frac{}{10}$

My Feelings Today.

5	
6	
7	
8	
9	
10	
11	
12pm	
1	
2	
3	
4	
5	
6	
8	

Extra Notes:

DATE:...............

SOMEONE THAT HELPED ME TODAY...

TODAY I FEEL:

THREE GOOD THINGS ABOUT TODAY....

1

2

3

ONE WORRY I HAVE IS....

I Score Today...

10

My Feelings Today

5	
6	
7	
8	
9	
10	
11	
12pm	
1	
2	
3	
4	
5	
6	
8	

Extra Notes:

DATE:...............

SOMEONE THAT HELPED ME TODAY...

TODAY I FEEL:

THREE GOOD THINGS ABOUT TODAY....

1

2

3

ONE WORRY I HAVE IS....

I Score Today...

10

My Feelings Today.

5	
6	
7	
8	
9	
10	
11	
12pm	
1	
2	
3	
4	
5	
6	
7	
8	

Extra Notes:

DATE:...............

SOMEONE THAT HELPED ME TODAY...

TODAY I FEEL:

THREE GOOD THINGS ABOUT TODAY....

1

2

3

ONE WORRY I HAVE IS....

I Score Today...

$\dfrac{\quad}{10}$

My Feelings Today.

5	
6	
7	
8	
9	
10	
11	
12pm	
1	
2	
3	
4	
5	
6	
7	
8	

Extra Notes:

DATE:...............

SOMEONE THAT HELPED ME TODAY...

THREE GOOD THINGS ABOUT TODAY....

1

2

3

ONE WORRY I HAVE IS....

I Score Today...

$\dfrac{\quad}{10}$

My Feelings Today

5	
6	
7	
8	
9	
10	
11	
12pm	
1	
2	
3	
4	
5	
6	
8	

Extra Notes:

DATE:...............

SOMEONE THAT HELPED ME TODAY...

THREE GOOD THINGS ABOUT TODAY....

1

2

3

ONE WORRY I HAVE IS.....

I Score Today...

10

My Feelings Today.

5	
6	
7	
8	
9	
10	
11	
12pm	
1	
2	
3	
4	
5	
6	
8	

Extra Notes:

DATE:..............

SOMEONE THAT HELPED
ME TODAY...

TODAY I FEEL:

THREE GOOD THINGS
ABOUT TODAY....

1

2

3

ONE WORRY I HAVE IS....

I Score Today...

$\dfrac{\quad}{10}$

My Feelings Today

5	
6	
7	
8	
9	
10	
11	
12pm	
1	
2	
3	
4	
5	
6	
7	
8	

Extra Notes:

DATE:..............

SOMEONE THAT HELPED ME TODAY...

THREE GOOD THINGS ABOUT TODAY....

1

2

3

ONE WORRY I HAVE IS....

I Score Today...

$\frac{}{10}$

My Feelings Today

5	
6	
7	
8	
9	
10	
11	
12pm	
1	
2	
3	
4	
5	
6	
7	
8	

Extra Notes:

DATE:...............

TODAY I FEEL:

SOMEONE THAT HELPED
ME TODAY...

THREE GOOD THINGS
ABOUT TODAY....

1

2

3

ONE WORRY I HAVE IS....

I Score Today...

$\overline{10}$

My Feelings Today.

5	
6	
7	
8	
9	
10	
11	
12pm	
1	
2	
3	
4	
5	
6	
7	
8	

Extra Notes:

DATE:...............

TODAY I FEEL:

SOMEONE THAT HELPED ME TODAY...

THREE GOOD THINGS ABOUT TODAY....

1

2

3

ONE WORRY I HAVE IS....

I Score Today...

—
10

My Feelings Today

5	
6	
7	
8	
9	
10	
11	
12pm	
1	
2	
3	
4	
5	
6	
8	

Extra Notes:

DATE:...............

TODAY I FEEL:

SOMEONE THAT HELPED ME TODAY...

THREE GOOD THINGS ABOUT TODAY....

1

2

3

ONE WORRY I HAVE IS....

I Score Today...

$\dfrac{}{10}$

My Feelings Today.

5	
6	
7	
8	
9	
10	
11	
12pm	
1	
2	
3	
4	
5	
6	
7	
8	

Extra Notes:

DATE:...............

SOMEONE THAT HELPED
ME TODAY...

THREE GOOD THINGS
ABOUT TODAY....

1

2

3

ONE WORRY I HAVE IS....

I Score Today...

$\dfrac{\quad}{10}$

My Feelings Today

5	
6	
7	
8	
9	
10	
11	
12pm	
1	
2	
3	
4	
5	
6	
8	

Extra Notes:

DATE:...............

SOMEONE THAT HELPED ME TODAY...

TODAY I FEEL:

THREE GOOD THINGS ABOUT TODAY....

1

2

3

ONE WORRY I HAVE IS....

I Score Today...

10

My Feelings Today

5	
6	
7	
8	
9	
10	
11	
12pm	
1	
2	
3	
4	
5	
6	
8	

Extra Notes:

DATE:...............

SOMEONE THAT HELPED
ME TODAY...

THREE GOOD THINGS
ABOUT TODAY....

1

2

3

ONE WORRY I HAVE IS....

I Score Today...

10

My Feelings Today

5	
6	
7	
8	
9	
10	
11	
12pm	
1	
2	
3	
4	
5	
6	
7	
8	

Extra Notes:

DATE:..............

SOMEONE THAT HELPED ME TODAY...

TODAY I FEEL:

THREE GOOD THINGS ABOUT TODAY....

1

2

3

ONE WORRY I HAVE IS....

I Score Today...

—
10

My Feelings Today.

5	
6	
7	
8	
9	
10	
11	
12pm	
1	
2	
3	
4	
5	
6	
8	

Extra Notes:

DATE:..............

SOMEONE THAT HELPED
ME TODAY...

TODAY I FEEL:

THREE GOOD THINGS
ABOUT TODAY....

1

2

3

ONE WORRY I HAVE IS....

I Score Today...

$\frac{\qquad}{10}$

My Feelings Today

5	
6	
7	
8	
9	
10	
11	
12pm	
1	
2	
3	
4	
5	
6	
7	
8	

Extra Notes:

DATE:...............

SOMEONE THAT HELPED ME TODAY...

THREE GOOD THINGS ABOUT TODAY....

1

2

3

TODAY I FEEL:

ONE WORRY I HAVE IS....

I Score Today...

10

My Feelings Today.

5	
6	
7	
8	
9	
10	
11	
12pm	
1	
2	
3	
4	
5	
6	
7	
8	

Extra Notes:

DATE:...............

SOMEONE THAT HELPED
ME TODAY...

THREE GOOD THINGS
ABOUT TODAY....

1

2

3

ONE WORRY I HAVE IS....

I Score Today...

10

My Feelings Today

5	
6	
7	
8	
9	
10	
11	
12pm	
1	
2	
3	
4	
5	
6	
8	

Extra Notes:

DATE:...............

SOMEONE THAT HELPED ME TODAY...

THREE GOOD THINGS ABOUT TODAY....

1

2

3

ONE WORRY I HAVE IS....

I Score Today...

10

My Feelings Today.

5	
6	
7	
8	
9	
10	
11	
12pm	
1	
2	
3	
4	
5	
6	
8	

Extra Notes:

DATE:...............

SOMEONE THAT HELPED ME TODAY...

TODAY I FEEL:

THREE GOOD THINGS ABOUT TODAY....

1

2

3

ONE WORRY I HAVE IS....

I Score Today...

$\dfrac{}{10}$

My Feelings Today

5	
6	
7	
8	
9	
10	
11	
12pm	
1	
2	
3	
4	
5	
6	
8	

Extra Notes:

DATE:................

SOMEONE THAT HELPED
ME TODAY...

TODAY I FEEL:

THREE GOOD THINGS
ABOUT TODAY....

1

2

3

ONE WORRY I HAVE IS....

I Score Today...

$\frac{}{10}$

My Feelings Today

5	
6	
7	
8	
9	
10	
11	
12pm	
1	
2	
3	
4	
5	
6	
8	

Extra Notes:

My Feelings Today

5	
6	
7	
8	
9	
10	
11	
12pm	
1	
2	
3	
4	
5	
6	
8	

Extra Notes:

DATE:..............

SOMEONE THAT HELPED ME TODAY...

TODAY I FEEL:

THREE GOOD THINGS ABOUT TODAY....

1

2

3

ONE WORRY I HAVE IS....

I Score Today...

$\frac{}{10}$

My Feelings Today

5	
6	
7	
8	
9	
10	
11	
12pm	
1	
2	
3	
4	
5	
6	
8	

Extra Notes:

DATE:..............

SOMEONE THAT HELPED
ME TODAY...

THREE GOOD THINGS
ABOUT TODAY....

1

2

3

ONE WORRY I HAVE IS....

I Score Today...

10

My Feelings Today.

5	
6	
7	
8	
9	
10	
11	
12pm	
1	
2	
3	
4	
5	
6	
8	

Extra Notes:

DATE:...............

SOMEONE THAT HELPED ME TODAY...

THREE GOOD THINGS ABOUT TODAY....

1

2

3

TODAY I FEEL:

ONE WORRY I HAVE IS....

I Score Today...

$\frac{}{10}$

My Feelings Today

5	
6	
7	
8	
9	
10	
11	
12pm	
1	
2	
3	
4	
5	
6	
7	
8	

Extra Notes:

DATE:..............

SOMEONE THAT HELPED ME TODAY...

TODAY I FEEL:

THREE GOOD THINGS ABOUT TODAY.....

1

2

3

ONE WORRY I HAVE IS.....

I Score Today...

$\frac{}{10}$

My Feelings Today

5	
6	
7	
8	
9	
10	
11	
12pm	
1	
2	
3	
4	
5	
6	
7	
8	

Extra Notes:

DATE:..............

SOMEONE THAT HELPED ME TODAY...

TODAY I FEEL:

THREE GOOD THINGS ABOUT TODAY....

1

2

3

ONE WORRY I HAVE IS....

I Score Today...

$\dfrac{}{10}$

My Feelings Today

5	
6	
7	
8	
9	
10	
11	
12pm	
1	
2	
3	
4	
5	
6	
7	
8	

Extra Notes:

DATE:...............

TODAY I FEEL:

SOMEONE THAT HELPED ME TODAY...

THREE GOOD THINGS ABOUT TODAY....

1

2

3

ONE WORRY I HAVE IS....

I Score Today...

10

My Feelings Today

5	
6	
7	
8	
9	
10	
11	
12pm	
1	
2	
3	
4	
5	
6	
8	

Extra Notes:

DATE:...............

SOMEONE THAT HELPED
ME TODAY...

TODAY I FEEL:

THREE GOOD THINGS
ABOUT TODAY....

1

2

3

ONE WORRY I HAVE IS....

I Score Today...

$\frac{}{10}$

My Feelings Today

5	
6	
7	
8	
9	
10	
11	
12pm	
1	
2	
3	
4	
5	
6	
8	

Extra Notes:

DATE:..............

SOMEONE THAT HELPED
ME TODAY...

TODAY I FEEL:

THREE GOOD THINGS
ABOUT TODAY....

1

2

3

ONE WORRY I HAVE IS....

I Score Today...

10

My Feelings Today.

5	
6	
7	
8	
9	
10	
11	
12pm	
1	
2	
3	
4	
5	
6	
7	
8	

Extra Notes:

DATE:...............

SOMEONE THAT HELPED ME TODAY...

TODAY I FEEL:

THREE GOOD THINGS ABOUT TODAY....

1

2

3

ONE WORRY I HAVE IS....

I Score Today...

$\overline{10}$

My Feelings Today

5	
6	
7	
8	
9	
10	
11	
12pm	
1	
2	
3	
4	
5	
6	
8	

Extra Notes:

DATE:...............

SOMEONE THAT HELPED ME TODAY...

TODAY I FEEL:

THREE GOOD THINGS ABOUT TODAY....

1

2

3

ONE WORRY I HAVE IS....

I Score Today...

10

My Feelings Today

5	
6	
7	
8	
9	
10	
11	
12pm	
1	
2	
3	
4	
5	
6	
8	

Extra Notes:

DATE:...............

SOMEONE THAT HELPED ME TODAY...

THREE GOOD THINGS ABOUT TODAY....

1

2

3

ONE WORRY I HAVE IS....

I Score Today...

$\dfrac{}{10}$

My Feelings Today

5	
6	
7	
8	
9	
10	
11	
12pm	
1	
2	
3	
4	
5	
6	
8	

Extra Notes:

DATE:...............

SOMEONE THAT HELPED ME TODAY...

TODAY I FEEL:

THREE GOOD THINGS ABOUT TODAY....

1

2

3

ONE WORRY I HAVE IS.....

I Score Today...

$\dfrac{\quad}{10}$

My Feelings Today

5	
6	
7	
8	
9	
10	
11	
12pm	
1	
2	
3	
4	
5	
6	
8	

Extra Notes:

DATE:..............

SOMEONE THAT HELPED ME TODAY...

THREE GOOD THINGS ABOUT TODAY....

1

2

3

ONE WORRY I HAVE IS....

I Score Today...

$\overline{10}$

My Feelings Today

5	
6	
7	
8	
9	
10	
11	
12pm	
1	
2	
3	
4	
5	
6	
7	
8	

Extra Notes:

DATE:..............

SOMEONE THAT HELPED ME TODAY...

THREE GOOD THINGS ABOUT TODAY....

1

2

3

ONE WORRY I HAVE IS....

I Score Today...

$\frac{}{10}$

My Feelings Today.

5	
6	
7	
8	
9	
10	
11	
12pm	
1	
2	
3	
4	
5	
6	
7	
8	

Extra Notes:

DATE:...............

TODAY I FEEL:

SOMEONE THAT HELPED
ME TODAY...

THREE GOOD THINGS
ABOUT TODAY....

1

2

3

ONE WORRY I HAVE IS....

I Score Today...

$\frac{}{10}$

My Feelings Today

5	
6	
7	
8	
9	
10	
11	
12pm	
1	
2	
3	
4	
5	
6	
8	

Extra Notes:

My Feelings Today

5	
6	
7	
8	
9	
10	
11	
12pm	
1	
2	
3	
4	
5	
6	
8	

Extra Notes:

DATE:...............

TODAY I FEEL:

SOMEONE THAT HELPED ME TODAY...

THREE GOOD THINGS ABOUT TODAY....

1

2

3

ONE WORRY I HAVE IS.....

I Score Today...

10

My Feelings Today

5	
6	
7	
8	
9	
10	
11	
12pm	
1	
2	
3	
4	
5	
6	
8	

Extra Notes:

DATE:...............

SOMEONE THAT HELPED ME TODAY...

THREE GOOD THINGS ABOUT TODAY....

1

2

3

ONE WORRY I HAVE IS....

I Score Today...

$\frac{}{10}$

My Feelings Today

5	
6	
7	
8	
9	
10	
11	
12pm	
1	
2	
3	
4	
5	
6	
8	

Extra Notes:

DATE:...............

TODAY I FEEL:

SOMEONE THAT HELPED ME TODAY...

THREE GOOD THINGS ABOUT TODAY....

1

2

3

ONE WORRY I HAVE IS....

I Score Today...

$\frac{}{10}$

My Feelings Today

5	
6	
7	
8	
9	
10	
11	
12pm	
1	
2	
3	
4	
5	
6	
7	
8	

Extra Notes:

DATE:...............

SOMEONE THAT HELPED ME TODAY...

TODAY I FEEL:

THREE GOOD THINGS ABOUT TODAY....

1

2

3

ONE WORRY I HAVE IS....

I Score Today...

$\dfrac{}{10}$

My Feelings Today

5	
6	
7	
8	
9	
10	
11	
12pm	
1	
2	
3	
4	
5	
6	
7	
8	

Extra Notes:

DATE:..............

TODAY I FEEL:

SOMEONE THAT HELPED ME TODAY...

THREE GOOD THINGS ABOUT TODAY....

1

2

3

ONE WORRY I HAVE IS....

I Score Today...

10

My Feelings Today.

5	
6	
7	
8	
9	
10	
11	
12pm	
1	
2	
3	
4	
5	
6	
8	

Extra Notes:

DATE:...............

SOMEONE THAT HELPED ME TODAY...

TODAY I FEEL:

THREE GOOD THINGS ABOUT TODAY....

1

2

3

ONE WORRY I HAVE IS....

I Score Today...

$\dfrac{}{10}$

My Feelings Today.

5	
6	
7	
8	
9	
10	
11	
12pm	
1	
2	
3	
4	
5	
6	
8	

Extra Notes:

DATE:...............

SOMEONE THAT HELPED ME TODAY...

THREE GOOD THINGS ABOUT TODAY....

1

2

3

ONE WORRY I HAVE IS....

I Score Today...

$\frac{}{10}$

My Feelings Today

5	
6	
7	
8	
9	
10	
11	
12pm	
1	
2	
3	
4	
5	
6	
8	

Extra Notes:

DATE:...............

SOMEONE THAT HELPED ME TODAY...

TODAY I FEEL:

THREE GOOD THINGS ABOUT TODAY....

1

2

3

ONE WORRY I HAVE IS....

I Score Today...

10

My Feelings Today

5	
6	
7	
8	
9	
10	
11	
12pm	
1	
2	
3	
4	
5	
6	
8	

Extra Notes:

DATE:...............

SOMEONE THAT HELPED ME TODAY...

TODAY I FEEL:

THREE GOOD THINGS ABOUT TODAY....

1

2

3

ONE WORRY I HAVE IS....

I Score Today...

$\overline{10}$

My Feelings Today

5
6
7
8
9
10
11
12pm
1
2
3
4
5
6
8